THE EASY PIANO COL
EARLY ROMANTIC

GOLD

Published by:
Chester Music Limited,
14-15 Berners Street, London W1T 3LJ, UK.

Exclusive Distributors:
Music Sales Limited,
Distribution Centre, Newmarket Road, Bury St Edmunds, Suffolk IP33 3YB, UK.
Music Sales Corporation,
257 Park Avenue South, New York, NY10010, United States of America.
Music Sales Pty Limited,
120 Rothschild Avenue, Rosebery, NSW 2018, Australia.

Order No. CH72325
ISBN 978-1-84772-054-2
This book © Copyright 2007 by Chester Music.

Compiled and edited by Jessica Williams.
Arranging and engraving supplied by Camden Music and Derek Jones.
Cover design by the Design Corporation.

Printed in the EU.

Your Guarantee of Quality:
As publishers, we strive to produce every book to the highest commercial standards.
The music has been freshly engraved and carefully designed to minimise
awkward page turns to make playing from it a real pleasure.
Particular care has been given to specifying acid-free, neutral-sized
paper made from pulps which have not been elemental chlorine bleached.
This pulp is from farmed sustainable forests and was produced
with special regard for the environment.
Throughout, the printing and binding have been planned to ensure a sturdy,
attractive publication which should give years of enjoyment.
If your copy fails to meet our high standards, please inform us and we will gladly replace it.

www.musicsales.com

CHESTER MUSIC
part of the Music Sales Group

London/New York/Paris/Sydney/Copenhagen/Berlin/Madrid/Tokyo

EARLY ROMANTICISM

Trying to define the word romanticism is almost as complicated as trying to understand its origins in early 19th-century art, literature and music. The beginnings of romanticism can be traced back to the first stirrings of the Enlightenment in the latter half of the 18th century and the widespread reading of the French philosopher Jean-Jacques Rousseau, with his emphasis on social justice, and his belief in integrity of the common man. The French Revolution of 1789 (itself partially inspired by Rousseau) gave rise to a new wave of liberal ideology and widespread political unrest. Young artists were thrilled by the new developments, and the early 1800s saw an explosion of new creative ideas.

It is important to stress that romanticism, by its very nature, is more of a spirit of the age than a coherent movement, and its characteristics vary considerably from country to country and from one artist to another. In Britain, romanticism tended to manifest itself in literature: the narrative poems of Byron and the novels of Walter Scott swept across Europe like wildfire. In Italy the new bel canto style of opera, full of vocal virtuosity and exaggerated theatrical effects, pioneered by Rossini, Bellini and Donizetti, became fabulously popular. In Germany, poets like Goethe and Schiller pointed the way to a new intellectual renaissance while Beethoven, with his radical symphonies of unprecedented scale and gravity trail-blazed a path into the new century. The tragedy of his deafness and the boldness of his artistic vision made him a kind of icon for subsequent generations of romantic composers.

Among the prevailing tendencies in romantic thinking there was a new emphasis on heightened emotion and the adventure of imagination. The 'cult of genius', the scorning of convention and the pre-eminence of originality were prized more highly than mere creative order and technical control. One might say that romanticism both grew out of and reacted against classicism and the Enlightenment: in the pursuit of liberty, both as a political and an artistic ideal, traditional forms gave way to new experimental ones. Artists began to turn away from rationalism (the keystone of the Enlightenment) towards the irrational, and to delight in subjects that would have previously been considered grotesque: at the first performance of Weber's opera *Der Freischütz* in 1821, members of the audience swooned at the orchestral depiction of sinister supernatural powers; Berlioz's *Symphonie fantastique* of 1830 depicts a world of opium-induced reveries culminating in a witches' Sabbath.

The cult of virtuosity was another hallmark of the early romantic era. The great Italian violinist Paganini (a friend and admirer of Berlioz) was considered so extraordinarily brilliant that his gifts were popularly thought to be demonic in origin. Meanwhile, a younger generation of pianist-composers came to prominence. In Germany, the young Robert Schumann had hoped to be a virtuoso pianist until he injured his hand with a homemade practicing contraption. Undaunted, he decided to compose for the instrument instead, and through the 1830s wrote a sequence of masterpieces. His wife, Clara (also a gifted composer) became one of the greatest pianists of her age. As a music journalist, Schumann was one of the first to notice the astonishing gifts of the polish composer, Frédéric Chopin, who concentrated his life's work into writing almost nothing but beautifully refined piano music. Most spectacular of all was the dazzling early career of Franz Liszt who toured Europe in the 1830s giving concerts of such spectacular virtuosity that he became one of the most celebrated men in Europe, internationally acclaimed for his musical genius and equally notorious for his colourful love-life.

The early romantic era was characterised by the development of new forms. Just as the leading early romantic painters, like Turner in Britain or Caspar David Friedrich in Germany, tended to paint landscapes pregnant with symbolic meaning, composers began to use freer forms to express a whole wealth of ideas. In Germany, composers like Schubert and Schumann pioneered the Song Cycle (a unified collection of songs bound together by a common mood or narrative), while Felix Mendelssohn—who sprang to prominence with a series of teenage compositions, even more prodigious than that of Mozart's half a century earlier—invented a new kind of piano piece called a '*Song without Words*' where melody was free to be expressive without the constraint of words. Berlioz and Liszt (inspired by literary models) developed new forms of Programme music—almost all their compositions express extra musical ideas, sometimes in the form of dramatic narratives. Liszt even invented a new term 'Tone Poem' to describe some of these compositions. Although traditional forms like sonatas and symphonies continued to be written, they were often invested with new programmatic meanings (as in Berlioz's *Harold en Italie* or Liszt's *Faust Symphony*), bound together by a recurring theme or idée fixe often representing a character or poetic idea.

However, it was in the operas of that greatest of egotists, Richard Wagner, that these tendencies reached their ultimate expression. Influenced by the innovations of Berlioz and Liszt (who was his father-in-law) he assigned specific themes to specific characters or emotions (called Leitmotifs). Wagner's works represent, not only in their subject matter, but also in their richness of harmony and their extraordinary orchestration, the climax of romanticism, not least in the most titanic work in musical history, *Der Ring des Nibelungen*.

EARLY ROMANTIC COMPOSERS

Hector Berlioz (1803–1869) was the son of a cultured doctor who imbued his son with a love for the classics (which bore fruit in Hector's most ambitious project, the monstrous opera, *The Trojans*, in 1858). After a period in Paris studying medicine, Berlioz decided to study composition at the Paris Conservatoire, where he eventually won the coveted Prix de Rome in 1830.

Berlioz had many talents and he earned his living as a witty and perceptive music critic. As a composer, his genius was closely linked to his love for and understanding of the orchestra and his scores reveal an astounding orchestral imagination, years ahead of their time.

Berlioz was, in many ways, the archetypal early romantic artist, blurring the traditional boundaries between concerto, opera and symphony, just as he blurred any distinction between his composition and his private life. His infatuation with the Irish actress Harriet Smithson caused him to woo her with such zeal that she eventually agreed to marry him though she spoke no French and he no English!

Georges Bizet (1838–1875) was born to a musical family and showed such prodigious talent that he was admitted to the Paris Conservatoire at the age of nine. While still a student he composed his brilliant and charming *Symphony in C*. In 1857, he won the Prix de Rome but thereafter, struggled to achieve recognition. In 1863, his opera *The Pearl Fishers* (1863), was poorly received and several other operatic ventures failed although Bizet won a measure of popularity with his music for Daudet's play *L'Arlésienne*.

Bizet's final opera, *Carmen* (1875) created a considerable scandal at its first performance at the *Opéra-Comique* in Paris, partly because of its risqué subject matter and tragic conclusion. Lambasted in the press, the strain proved too much for Bizet who died three months later aged 36. *Carmen* has since proved to be the most popular opera in the repertoire.

Alexander Borodin (1833–1887) was one of the most brilliant men of the 19th century. The son of a Georgian prince, he spoke several languages and was accomplished on a number of instruments. In 1858 he completed his doctoral dissertation in medicine and became a professor of chemistry at the St. Petersburg Academy. He established an international reputation as a scientist (a chemical reaction was named after him) and was a noted philanthropist, championing women's rights and other important causes.

As a composer, he managed to complete two symphonies, a pair of magnificent string quartets and a 'symphonic sketch', *In the Steppes of Central Asia*. As a member of the composers group known as 'The Five', each Borodin work was eagerly awaited, none more so than his epic opera, *Prince Igor*, which remained unfinished at his death.

Frédéric Chopin (1810–1849) was a child prodigy in Warsaw and found himself much in demand in aristocratic households. His virtuosity on the piano was only matched by his early brilliance as a composer. In 1831 he moved to Paris, where he was again much in demand as a society pianist and teacher. His *Etudes Op.10* (1832) created a new standard for pianistic technique.

Nearly all of Chopin's mature compositions are masterpieces for piano solo. They demonstrate extraordinary boldness of harmony, scintillating piano writing, melodic grace and perfection of form. Chopin's influence was immense. His private life was rather unsatisfactory. His ten-year relationship with the novelist George Sand ended unhappily in 1847. He composed little thereafter.

Léo Delibes (1836–1891) studied organ at the Paris Conservatoire before turning his hand to writing operettas in the style of Offenbach. Thereafter, he concentrated on ballet, writing three fine works in that genre—*La Source* (1866), *Coppélia* (1870) and *Sylvia* (1876). The latter was much admired by Tchaikovsky.

Delibes' later operas, *Le Roi l'a dit* (1873) and *Lakmé* (composed in the then fashionable 'French Oriental' style), were huge successes. Delibes' genius was always for lightness of touch, melodic grace and orchestral delicacy. Elgar once claimed that he learnt more about composition from looking at scores of Delibes than he ever did from studying Wagner.

César Franck (1822–1890) was born in Belgium but spent most of his life in Paris. He excelled at the Paris Conservatoire and became well known as an organ virtuoso. His six pieces for organ made a deep impression on Liszt when he heard Franck perform them in 1866.

In 1872 Franck was appointed professor of organ at the conservatoire. His many famous pupils revered him for his kind and simple nature, which earned him the nickname 'Père Franck'. His greatest works include a violin sonata, a symphony, a string quartet and various piano and organ pieces, all written in a learned but daringly rich harmonic idiom. Tragically, he died after being run over by a horse-drawn bus.

Franz Liszt (1811–1886) was a larger-than-life figure on the landscape of 19th-century music—he was the greatest piano virtuoso of his age and consequently the greatest travelling celebrity (the term 'Lisztomania' was coined to describe audiences' response to his playing). As a composer of piano music, he discovered undreamt sonorities and techniques, a wealth of new harmonic innovations, and learnt from his friend Berlioz new ways of structuring music around literary models.

Liszt was, in every sense, a radical for whom music was a grand and passionate adventure. In addition to his vast range of compositions for piano, his orchestral tone poems were enormously influential in the 19th century.

Felix Mendelssohn (1809–1847) was the grandson of the Jewish philosopher, Moses Mendelssohn. From early on, the young Felix displayed exceptional musical gifts. The precocious genius of his compositions up to and including the masterly *Octet*, written at the age of 16, and the overture to *A Midsummer Night's Dream* the following year, is unequalled in the history of western music.

Mendelssohn's later music was no less accomplished—his concert overtures and four symphonies are flawlessly executed, as is his magnificent *Violin Concerto* of 1844. He died of a brain haemorrhage at the age of 37. Schumann described him as the Mozart of his age.

Modest Mussorgsky (1839–1881) was one of Russia's most original composers. Born into a noble family, he showed remarkable talent as a child, performing a piano concerto in public at the age of nine.

For a brief period Mussorgsky became an army officer before resigning his commission in the order to become a composer. He joined the influential group of Russian nationalist composers, later known as 'The Five', and devoted himself to forging an authentic Russian style.

His greatest achievement was the opera *Boris Godunov* in which he discovered a new declamatory style, quite different from anything in traditional opera. The opera's overwhelming choral scenes resulted in a triumphant première in 1874 but Mussorgsky's last years were a tragic spiral of alcoholism and debt. His piano masterpiece *Pictures At An Exhibition* was later orchestrated by Ravel.

Jacques Offenbach (1819–1880) was a French composer of German-Jewish origin. He studied cello at the Paris Conservatoire and travelled Europe as a virtuoso cellist, even performing to Queen Victoria at Windsor Castle in 1844. In 1850 he became a conductor at the Theatre Français and, five years later, set up his own theatre company for which he composed a series of outstandingly successful operettas, starting with *Orpheus in the Underworld* (1858).

Offenbach's operettas became famous in Vienna and London (where they influenced the later work of Gilbert and Sullivan). However, due to financial mismanagement, his company went bankrupt in the 1870s. Undaunted, he went on to compose his final masterpiece, the large-scale fantasy opera *The Tales of Hoffmann*.

Franz Schubert (1797–1828) was one of the greatest composers of the 19th century. Born in Vienna, the son of a schoolmaster, his early years were phenomenally productive. By the age of 18 he had composed six operas, three piano sonatas, three string quartets, four masses and five symphonies, all of which displayed his total mastery of the Viennese classical style. But it was in the 300 or more songs from the same period that his romantic imagination began to burgeon most powerfully.

Schubert's later years were even more extraordinary—the *'Trout' Quintet* (1819) and *Octet* (1824) are charming romantic serenades, his *Quartetsatz* (1821) and *Symphony No.8* (both mysteriously unfinished) are works of rich imagination and brooding passion. The masterpieces from his final years include the *'Great' Symphony No.9*, the song-cycle *Winterreise*, the final quartets and piano sonatas, and the incomparable *String Quintet*. He died at the age of 31.

Robert Schumann (1810–1856) was one of the leading composers of the romantic era. His early piano music (he composed exclusively for the piano in the 1830s) is remarkable for its poetic quality and matchless imagination. During this period Schumann established himself as a leading critic in Germany.

In 1840, following his marriage to the virtuoso pianist and composer, Clara Wieck, Schumann composed nothing but songs of unsurpassed beauty. To this one year belong his great song cycles *Dichterliebe*, *Myrthen* and *Frauenliebe und Leben*. In 1841 he composed nothing but orchestral music (including his lyrical piano concerto), and in 1842 nothing but chamber music. Such was the obsessive but profoundly fruitful nature of his genius. Sadly, Schumann's last years were marred by periods of insanity. He died in an asylum aged 46.

Johann Strauss I (1804–49) was the father of a dynasty of Viennese composers who raised dance music to the level of art. Strauss' music, especially his waltzes, made 19th-century Vienna the dancing capital of the world.

It is difficult for us now to imagine the revolutionary impact Strauss' waltzes made in the 1830s. With their rhythmic inventiveness and witty instrumental effects they attracted the attention of advanced musicians like Berlioz, who praised them in his memoirs.

Strauss' achievement was surpassed by that of his son, whose waltzes have proved more enduringly popular. However, the older composer's *Radetzky March* is still frequently played.

Richard Wagner (1813–1883) was obsessed from an early age with the synthesis of music and theatre. From his early career as a provincial opera conductor, to his world fame as creator of the *Ring Cycle*, his life was consumed with this obsession.

From his early successes with *Rienzi* and *The Flying Dutchman* through to the masterpieces of his later years, *Tristan and Isolde*, *The Mastersingers of Nurenburg* and *Parsifal*, Wagner honed his craft to the point of perfection. In the process, he created a musical style that was richer in its implications and more influential than that of any of his contemporaries.

Wagner always wrote his own words and developed a new kind of seamless musical landscape to accompany them. His theatrical ideals, which led to the building of his ideal theatre at Bayreuth, paved the way for cinematography. He was ruthless and self-centred in the pursuit of his ideals but the greatness of his work is nevertheless astounding.

Dance of The Sylphs
(from 'La damnation de Faust')

Composed by Hector Berlioz

Moderato

Au fond du temple saint
(Duet from 'The Pearl Fishers')

Composed by Georges Bizet

Ave Maria

Composed by Franz Schubert

Adagio

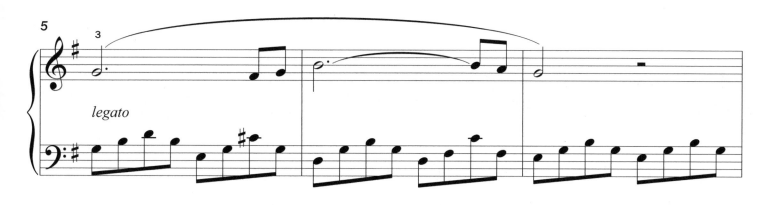

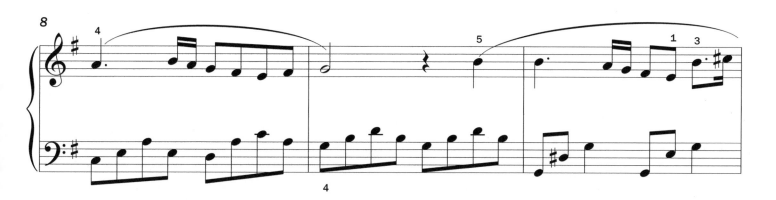

Barcarolle
(from 'Les contes d'Hoffmann')

Composed by Jacques Offenbach

The Can-Can
(from 'La Gaîté Parisienne')

Composed by Jacques Offenbach

Entr'acte
(from 'Rosamunde')

Composed by Franz Schubert

Flower Duet
(from 'Lakmé')

Composed by Léo Delibes

Andantino con moto

Habañera: 'L'amour est un oiseau rebelle'
(from 'Carmen')

Composed by Georges Bizet

*original rhythm

Liebesträume No.3
(Dream of Love)

Composed by Franz Liszt

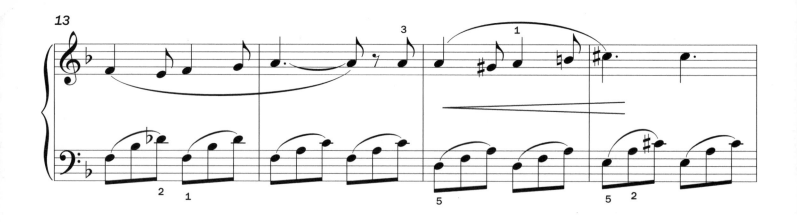

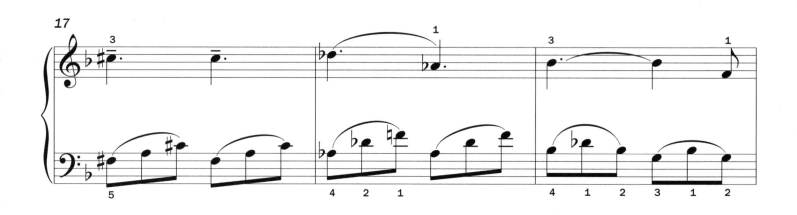

rit.

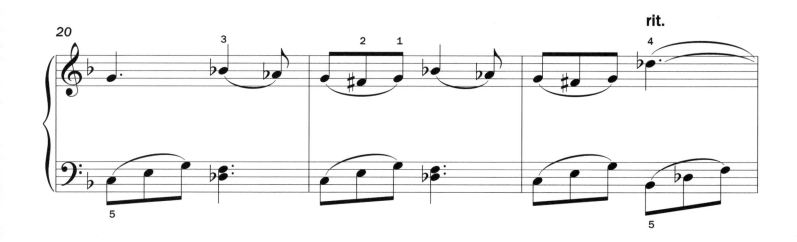

a tempo

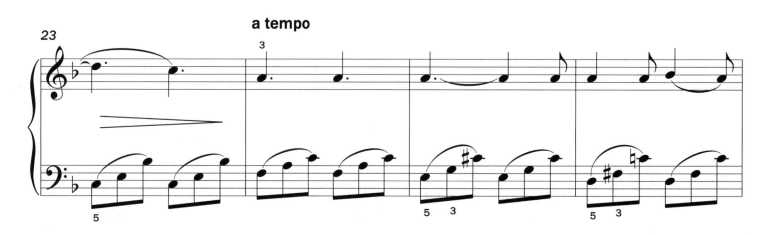

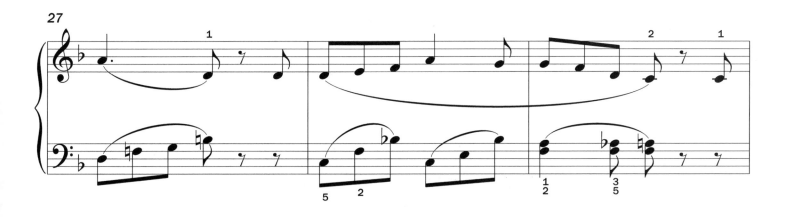

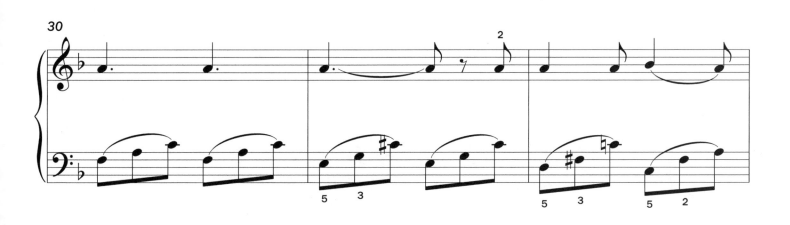

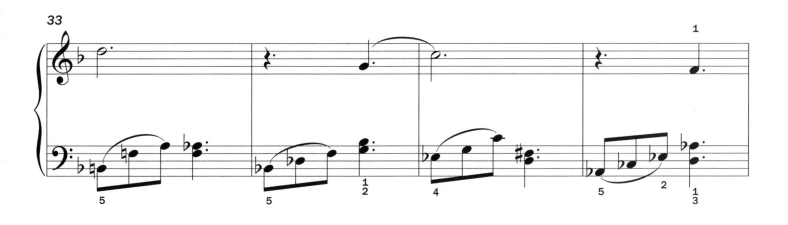

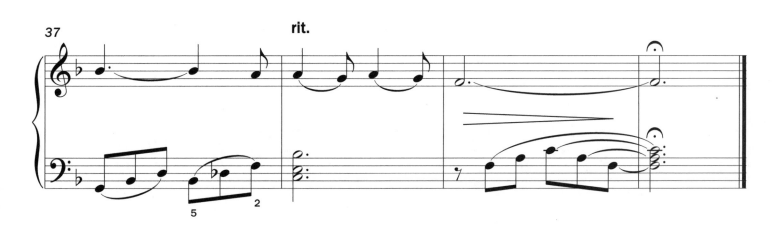

Impromptu No.3
Op.142

Composed by Franz Schubert

Nocturne
(from 'String Quartet No.2')

Composed by Alexander Borodin

Panis Angelicus

Composed by César Franck

rall. al fine

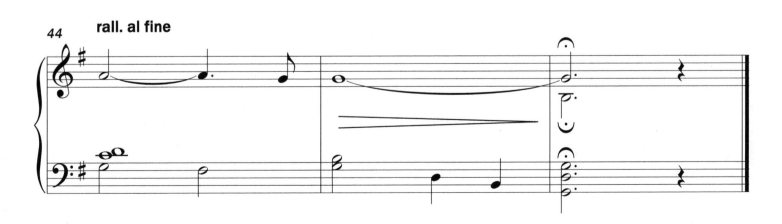

O, for the Wings of a Dove
(from 'Hear my prayer')

Composed by Felix Mendelssohn

Prelude
Op.2, No.4

Composed by Georges Bizet

Allegretto

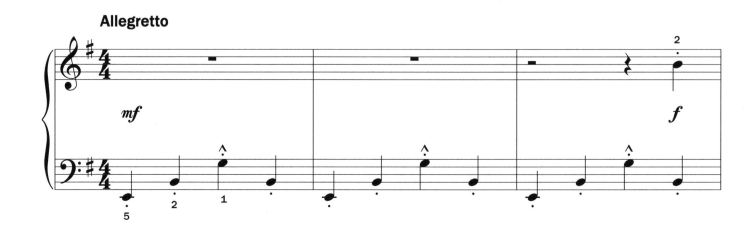

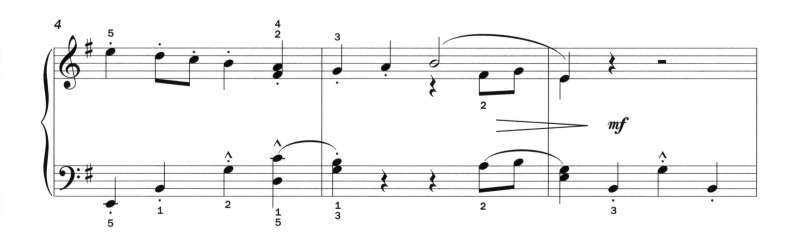

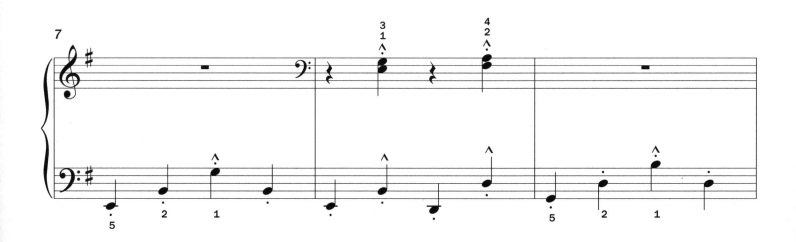

Prelude in D♭ major 'Raindrop'
Op.28, No.15

Composed by Frédéric Chopin

Prelude in E minor 'Suffocation'
Op.28, No.4

Composed by Frédéric Chopin

Promenade
(from 'Pictures At An Exhibition')

Composed by Modest Mussorgsky

Allegro giusto, nel modo Russico, senza allegreza, ma poco sostenuto

allargando

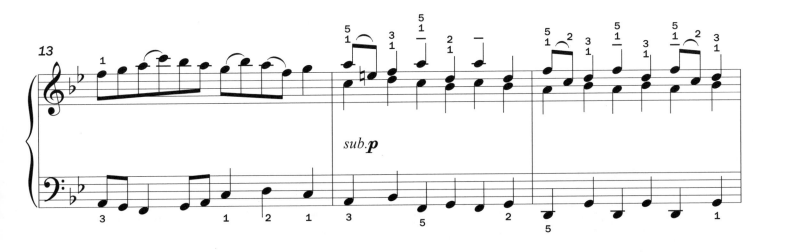

*sub.***p**

f

(f)

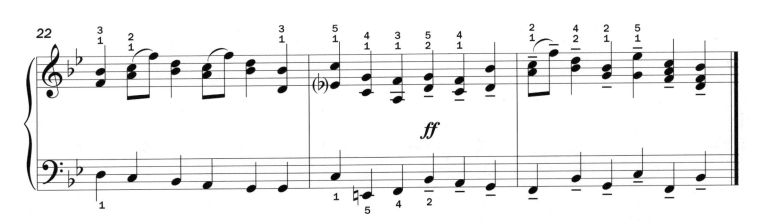

ff

Radetsky March

Composed by Johann Strauss I

Rakoczy March

Composed by Franz Liszt

Allegro deciso ed energico assai

D.C. al Coda

Coda

51

The Ride Of The Valkyries
(from 'Die Walküre')

Composed by Richard Wagner

Symphony No.3 'Scottish'
(1st movement theme)

Composed by Felix Mendelssohn

Andante con moto

Allegro un poco agitato

Tempo primo

D.S. al Fine

To The Evening Star
(from 'Tannhäuser')

Composed by Richard Wagner

Andante moderato

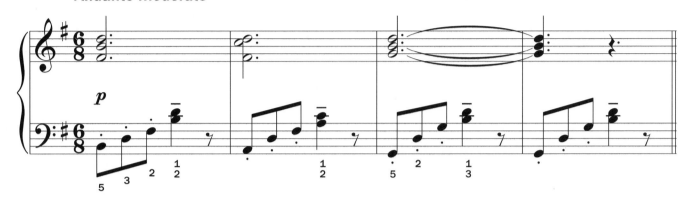

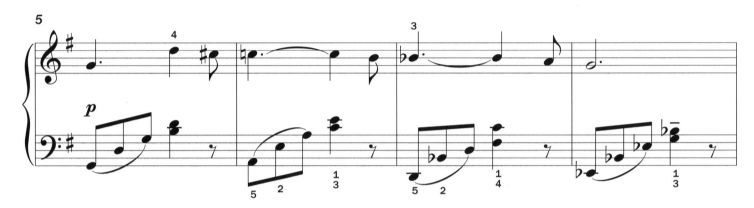

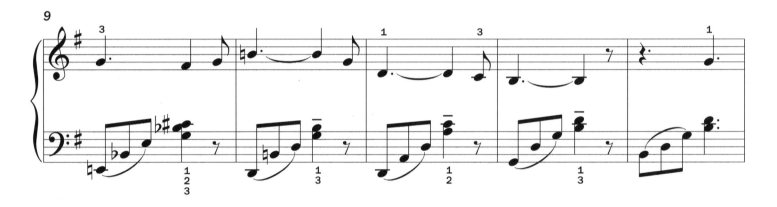

Träumerei
(from 'Kinderszenen')

Composed by Robert Schumann

Valse Lente
(from 'Coppélia')

Composed by Léo Delibes

Tempo di valse moderato

Trout Quintet
Op.114 (4th movement: Andantino)

Composed by Franz Schubert

123456789